Desperate Measures

Mylia Ashton

Published by Colors of Love, 2024.

Sign up for Mylia's mailing list[1] to receive notification of new releases, ARC opportunities, and other limited communications. Don't worry. Your information is safe and will never be shared.

This book was previously published under a different title.

---

1.   https://subscribeto.eo.page/myliaashton

Desperate Measures

Mylia Ashton

Blurb

FELICIA IS TRAPPED with no good solution. She wants her boss, Clayton, but she also needs the money his rich, snobby father offers her to disappear from his son's life. Reluctantly, she takes the money, but before she can leave, Clayton discovers what she's done. His passion for her only just exceeds his anger with her, and he demands she pay him back every cent of the money he reimbursed his father—in his bed and subject to his every whim. She's quickly falling for her handsome white boss, but his low opinion of her and refusal to hear her motives makes her certain there can never be anything but vitriol and desire between them.

Chapter One

FELICIA REENTERED HER office at Witherspoon's clutching a bag of Thai takeout from a nearby restaurant. A drizzling of rain had left her previously straightened hair a mass of kinky curls, and she ran a hand through it in an attempt to restore some semblance of order after setting lunch on her desk. It was hopeless, and she made a mental note to schedule a Brazilian blowout ASAP.

She took time to remove her raincoat, stow her purse in the bottom drawer of her desk and check the voicemail for messages before picking up the bag and moving to Clayton's office. A soft tap elicited an, "Enter," in his deep, New England baritone, and she opened the door.

Clayton looked up, his eyes gleaming darkly behind the silver frames of his reading glasses. The amber glow from the lamp on his desk brought out rich blue highlights in his black hair, making it difficult for Felicia to focus on the task he had set for her. She stood stupidly in the doorway, unable to tear her eyes from her boss.

A lock of hair flipped onto his forehead made her fingers itch to push it back, before proceeding down his face, to lightly caress the slight lines at his eyes. She would then move downward, across the strong bridge of his nose, to savor the firm texture of his full lips, before touching the slight cleft in his chin. Once her hands had explored the strong column of his throat, she would splay them across his chest as she sank onto his lap, her lips moist and ready to taste his....

Clayton clearing his throat brought her back to reality. With a shake of her head, Felicia did her best to hide her embarrassment at slipping into the fantasy. She lifted the bag higher. "Pad thai and green papaya salad, as requested."

He removed his glasses, setting them atop the file in one movement, even as he beckoned her forward with his other hand. Felicia's feet propelled her toward him, the heels of her shoes sinking into the frosted-gray carpet that was so plush it was probably more comfortable to sleep on than her own bed.

Upon reaching his desk, she put down the bag, opened it, and began removing the boxes. Each one was marked, so it was a simple matter to separate his order from hers. Silence filled the room while she completed the task, and Felicia tried to pretend she wasn't aware of Clayton's eyes sweeping over her as she worked. It was a difficult charade to maintain, since she could almost feel his sensual gaze touching her, caressing her intimately.

He wanted her as much as she wanted him. She was convinced they were both aware of the smoldering magnetism that arced between them whenever they shared the same space. Felicia knew enough about men to read the awareness in his eyes, to pick up on his subtle signals. She wasn't naïve enough to think Clayton lacked any experience with female companions, so she couldn't delude herself into thinking he didn't know she was equally attracted to him. The three months she had worked for him had only increased her attraction and, judging from recent behavior, his too.

Felicia's hands trembled slightly when she picked up the two boxes containing her order, along with a plastic fork, preparing to return to her desk. She held her breath, tensing as Clayton slid away from his desk to gain his feet. Her heart hammered in her ears when he walked toward her. She held breath escaped in a harsh exhalation when he brushed against her arm in the process of pointing to the cozy arrangement of a sofa, two chairs and a coffee table in the corner of his office.

"Stay, and have lunch with me."

Was she imagining the hint of smokiness in his tone? Felicia tried to appear nonchalant when she asked, "Shall I fetch the recorder?" The only times he had asked her to join him before had entailed working lunches, where he dictated memos into the recorder, or they discussed various strategies for dealing with a particular situation.

Clayton shook his head, scooped up his containers, and walked toward the sofa. His broad shoulders and lean waist, emphasized by the expertly tailored suit, drew her eyes, and it was all she could do not to fling herself at him.

With the fervent hope lunch was only foreplay, that finally some progress would take place today, leading them toward the seemingly inevitable affair, Felicia followed. Clayton had selected a middle cushion on the long sofa, and she sat beside him. The distance she left was enough to be provocative, but not completely blatant.

It took seconds to open her boxes, leaving her uncomfortably aware of his proximity and her lack of sparkling conversation. Being so close to him wasn't that unusual. After all, they worked together every day, usually in the confines of this office. But it was different today. Tension hung between them, and awareness of each other, of how easy it would be to lock the door and make love.

Or maybe she was imagining it all, Felicia wondered with a frown when Clayton leaned back and began eating. His posture suggested relaxation, without a hint of tension or suppressed awareness of her as more than his personal assistant. Had she manufactured in her own mind the exchanged glances that spoke of mutual longing? Was she so desperate for this man's touch that she was allowing herself to believe he was equally needy for hers?

Second-guessing her interpretation of his signals, Felicia absently picked at jasmine rice. As the silence stretched, her confidence grew shakier by the moment, until she was convinced she had imagined any sort of interest from her boss.

Panic took hold, and she buried the fork into the box and scooted away from him, ready to launch herself from the sofa and as far away from him as possible. Her face burned with humiliation, and she was desperate to escape. Silently, Felicia cursed Clayton when he finally decided to break the silence.

"What is it?" As he asked the question, Clayton grasped her forearm, his palm burning through the thin layer of silk separating them.

Felicia gasped when he rubbed a slow circle across her dark chocolate skin while turning her to face him. Her knees rested against his with the new position, and she had nowhere to look except into his eyes. They smoldered with banked desire. Her plump lips parted in response to his when she saw them forming a bow. Anticipation quickened her pulse and she arched forward, lifting her chin to facilitate the first meeting of their mouths.

She could already taste Clayton, had done so in countless nighttime fantasies, and it took every ounce of self-control to allow him to set the pace. He would appreciate that, since she suspected he enjoyed control in the bedroom as much as the boardroom.

His head lowered at a steady pace, and she waited impatiently. Her deep brown eyes closed when he got close enough for his breath to wash across her cheek. She curled her hands into fists in her lap to resist the urge to bury them into his hair and drag his mouth to hers.

Just as his lips were close enough for her to flick out her tongue to taste, the door opened without so much as a knock. A sound akin to a sob of frustration escaped Felicia, drowned out by the mechanical hum of George Witherspoon's wheelchair as it glided across the thick carpet.

His blue eyes raked over her, leaving Felicia exposed and raw, feeling as though he had measured her worth in a single glance and found her lacking. She leapt to her feet, counseling herself to act as though nothing unusual had been about to happen, even as she did her best to avoid the cold gaze of Clayton's father. "If you don't need me for anything else, Mr. Witherspoon, I'll leave you."

Clayton got to his feet slowly, his demeanor one of complete calm, as opposed to the one she feared she projected—guilt, though she had done nothing wrong. "That will be all, Ms. Calder."

She didn't miss the slight emphasis he placed on her surname. He seemed to want to remind her they had been on a first-name basis since her second week of employment. Was he exasperated by the way she had reacted to his father's unexpected entrance?

Felicia forced herself to walk steadily toward the door, holding her breath when she made it past George with little more than a sideways glance and dip of her head. Freedom from his contemptuous gaze was within sight when his voice froze her in place. "Just a moment, Miss Calder. I would like you to stay." Each word was issued coldly.

Somehow she swallowed the lump in her throat and managed a brittle smile when she turned to face George. Had she been braver, she would have pointed out she didn't answer to him, but all she managed was a limp, "Of course, sir."

It was as if he had read her unspoken thoughts. "How long have you been in my employ?"

"Three months."

George transferred his haughty gaze from her to his son. "You've lowered your standards, Clayton."

Felicia took a step back in reaction to the denouncement, even as Clayton moved toward his father, bridging the distance between them until he stood less than a foot behind her.

"You have no knowledge of what I look for in a personal assistant, nor of Felicia's qualifications, Father, so leave the hiring of my assistants to me," he said in a neutral tone, though his words had been a reproof of sorts. "Now, what brings you barging into my office?"

His father ignored the light reprimand and attempted turn of topic. "When I agreed to let you step in to my position, I expected you to maintain the company as I would have done. A pretty face is no excuse for a lapse in judgment."

Felicia gasped, but Clayton countered in a calm tone. "You hardly allowed me to take over willingly, Father." It was no secret George's stroke had left him incapacitated for months, forcing him to let his son finally have some real power in the company or risk losing everything to their competitors. She knew from Clayton—and from the old man's own behavior—that three years later, he was still bitter about no longer being in charge.

"That was a mistake that can be rectified. I'll remove you before you harm the company."

Clayton's cheeks flushed red, and a hint of annoyance appeared in his expression. She held her breath, wondering if she would witness an explosion of anger. Clayton had always been even-tempered and basically good-humored with her, but he had a reputation for being cold and calculating in business, with a hard edge reserved only for those who were dishonest in their dealings with the Witherspoon International.

His voice was soft, with only a subtle sibilance revealing the depths of his emotions. "Would you please leave us, Felicia?"

She might have remembered to nod as she scurried from the office, carefully avoiding George's eyes. Had the other man tried to call her back, she would have ignored his summons this time, having no desire to witness the argument between the two of them.

Out of habit, she closed the door behind her and went to her desk. Felicia sank into the chair, staring worriedly at the mahogany barrier separating her from Clayton and his father. In the three months she had worked for Clayton, twice before had she overheard him and his father arguing, both times via the phone, and had been privy only to Clayton's side.

Today was no different, except she could hear George's voice responding to his even tones. It carried over Clayton's, leaving no doubt to the extent of his rage. His pitch escalated with every exchange, until she could hear each syllable he spoke. If he hadn't been so enraged that he was speaking too rapidly for her to catch everything, she would have known exactly what he said.

Not that I need a transcript, she thought with a grimace. There was no mystery regarding the reason behind their exchange. Her. Clearly, the old man didn't approve of her, but Clayton was refusing to kowtow to his demands to get rid of her. At least Felicia hoped she was correctly interpreting the argument. Was it silly to have so much faith in him, to believe so firmly he would defend her to his father?

The office door opening, followed by George's chair whirring through it, broke her musings. She looked up, flinching at the derogatory glare the old man shot her way. Hands clutched in her lap, she stared at him without speaking as he negotiated his way toward the door that would lead him from their office suite to the main hall. She held her breath as he neared the door, daring to hope she would escape any further exchanges with him.

At the doorway, his glower deepened. "Don't get too comfortable behind that desk, Miss Calder."

When he was gone, she breathed a sigh of relief. It was difficult to take his parting words seriously when she knew Clayton must have refused to dismiss her. After her last disaster of a job, she couldn't stand the thought of being fired and forced to seek new employment with an even larger gap in her work history.

That, and she didn't want to leave so abruptly without finding out how things would turn out between herself and Clayton. Felicia groaned at the small voice that insisted on pointing out such thoughts. She schooled her expression into one of professional detachment when Clayton entered her office.

The tense arrangement of his features suggested he still bore anger from the exchange with his father, but he sounded as calm as ever when he spoke. "As soon as you've finished lunch, I'd like the Sterling file on my desk."

"Right away." Felicia managed a weak smile. "I've lost my appetite."

He nodded, his expression softening slightly. "As have I." With a single nod, he returned to his office.

She watched him go, attempting to suppress her disappointment. They had been so close to acting on their attraction. If not for George's intervention, they might be entangled in a passionate embrace this very second.

A long sigh escaped her when she left her desk to fetch the requested file. Maybe it was for the best. She knew firsthand how difficult it could be to work alongside someone whose attraction was out in the open. She didn't need that kind of scenario again. Yes, she had learned her lesson about office relationships working with Marco Trivanni.

That treacherous voice in the back of her mind insisted on tormenting her again by posing a question she was unable to banish from her mind for the rest of the afternoon. If she really intended to avoid an affair with Clayton, why was she still imagining what it would be like to make love with her boss?

FELICIA HADN'T REALIZED how on-edge she had been until she left Witherspoon's later that afternoon. As soon as her sensible sedan cleared the underground parking garage, she exhaled and her stiff shoulders relaxed. The events of the afternoon had cast a pall over both of them. She just hadn't allowed herself to acknowledge the new level of tension between her and Clayton until safely away from his presence.

She pointed her car in the direction of her sister's dorm, though all she really wanted to do was go home to a hot bath and try to pretend the day hadn't turned out as it had. She didn't want to feel uncomfortable around Clayton, but he had seemed to avoid her for the remainder of the afternoon. If she had to identify the reason, she might have tentatively settled on embarrassment from George's behavior, but that wasn't quite right. Had she imagined the flashes of guilt she seemed to read in his expression the few times work had necessitated they interact?

As she approached the two-story building one block from Tanja's college campus, Felicia tried to force the thoughts from her mind. Her distress would transmit easily to her sister, and she didn't need to pick up on her negative emotions. Tanja needed positive support for the forthcoming doctor's appointment.

Tanja was waiting for her at the entrance to the building, conversing with a fellow student. He was a handsome young man, with sunglasses that gave his face a lean, sexy look.

Felicia honked twice, and Tanja waved in her direction. She held her breath as her little sister negotiated the stairs with careless confidence. It took every fiber in her being not to get out and guide her sister to the car as Tanja tapped out the path with the white cane in her hands. Though she had only been using the cane for a few months, it seemed a natural extension of her body. Felicia wished she had adapted as well to the quick deterioration of her sister's eyesight as Tanja had. It was still in her to protect her from everything that could pose a danger, but her sister preferred to do things on her own.

Once she was settled into the passenger seat and safely belted in, Felicia let out the breath she had been holding, greeted her sister, and turned the car in the direction of Tanja's ophthalmologist. As she drove the few blocks to his office, they chatted about Tanja's latest class.

Felicia was thankful she didn't ask about work since Tanja had an uncanny knack to pick up on the slightest change in tone. Her sister loved to tease her about her "crush" on Clayton, and Felicia was in no mood to evade or deny the teasing allegations today. Nor did she want to relate what had happened with George, knowing it would outrage her little sister. She needed to keep her stress levels down.

Parking was tight, but Felicia angled into a spot on the street. She bit her tongue to avoid uttering a protest when Tanja bounded from the car before she had even finished parallel parking.

"I'll see you in there."

"Okay." Felicia waited until Tanja cleared the curb before angling her car the rest of the way into the space. She might have watched her sister until she made it inside the office if not for an impatient honk behind her. As she turned off the ignition, her cell phone beeped to alert her to an incoming text message.

After assuring herself Tanja had made it inside, Felicia retrieved the phone from the pocket on her purse and flipped it open. In two seconds, she had the message on her screen.

Felicia, come in ASAP. Major crisis with Sterling merger.

Experiencing a twinge of guilt, Felicia closed the phone without answering Clayton's summons. It was clear he needed her, but Tanja needed her more right then.

By the time she entered the ophthalmologist's office, Tanja was already on her way back. Felicia slipped in behind her sister and the nurse. As they went into the back office, she winced at the sight of a new painting hanging on the wall. Tanja would have loved the pixilated painting of a floral arrangement partially obscuring a Victorian maiden, if only she could have seen it.

Felicia tried to cling to hope as they were ushered into an exam room. Maybe her sister would one day see again and be able to have a normal life, to finish her studies in art history and re-enroll in a regular university, instead of the one she currently attended, tailored for the needs of the blind and visually impaired.

Dr. Batts's arrival interrupted her private thoughts, and she managed a smile for the middle-aged man. He took time to shake both their hands and exchange small talk before performing a brief exam on Tanja. Felicia held her breath when he sat down on a stool and opened the file on the counter.

"Last week's test results are back. Nothing's changed, Tanja." He sounded genuinely regretful. "The vision in your right eye remains at 20/400 and 20/600 in your left."

"So, no further degeneration then?" Tanja asked with false cheer.

Felicia easily detected the disappointment in her sister's airy tone. "But no improvement."

"There wouldn't be, Ms. Calder. As I've explained, Retinitis Pigmentosa doesn't spontaneously regress. All we can hope to do is halt the progress of the degeneration of the retina." Dr. Batts shook his bald head. "There isn't a cure."

"There must be something you can do. Tanja is young. Her vision has only been affected for the last year or so."

"She's only noticed symptoms for the past year. The RP has been destroying her retinal cells since the day she was born." A sigh escaped the ophthalmologist. "The only possible cure remains the procedure I've discussed with you before, and the odds aren't that favorable."

Felicia nodded, feeling a familiar sense of defeat crushing her. The cost of enrolling Tanja in the clinical trial through a private facility in Boston was astronomical. Even if they could somehow convince the clinic to take Tanja without cost, her sister would still need full living expenses and medical assistance during the months of treatment. She just couldn't afford it.

She tuned out the doctor as he and Tanja wrapped up the appointment. It took every ounce of willpower not to cry when she walked beside her sister a few minutes later, subtly guiding her to the car.

"I feel like pizza," said Tanja as she slipped into the car. Her hand unerringly found the seat belt, and she seemed to function as well without her sight as she had with it, but Felicia knew the toll it had taken on her to lose her sight so rapidly.

"Sorry, kiddo, but I have to go back to the office. You can order in, can't you?"

Tanja frowned at her when she had settled behind the steering wheel. "You work too much, sis." She shrugged. "Well, next time. You can drop me at Mario's on your way back to Witherspoon's."

"That's so far from your dorm."

"Six blocks. I think I can cover that distance without dropping from exhaustion." The dry note in her voice did little to cover the exasperation Tanja was trying to mask.

"What if you get lost?"

"I won't."

"You could be injured—"

"Enough," she said sharply. "God, Felicia, you're my sister, not my keeper. I'll be fine."

Felicia bit her tongue, managing a tight, "Okay." She understood Tanja's need for independence, but couldn't stop worrying about her. It had become habit to take care of her sister since their parents died, and having her sister go blind in the span of a year didn't make it easier to let go of her responsibilities.

Tanja didn't speak again until she pulled up in front of the kitschy pizza parlor. Her tone was light and mellow, the same as always. "Thanks for the ride."

She struggled to match it. "Sure." A husky note entered her voice. "Take care."

"I will." Unexpectedly, Tanja leaned over to press a kiss on her cheek. "You take care as well."

"I don't think dealing with merger issues will endanger me."

"But resisting your boss's charms might." With a giggle, Tanja made her escape from the car before Felicia could respond.

She accomplished the drive back to the office in good time. Her mind continued to worry at how to get Tanja into the trial, but she forced herself to focus on the Sterling merger and everything about it she could recall while swiping her card to enter the building. The elevator ferried her to the top floor quickly, and by the time she stepped out, she had on a professional face.

As she walked down the marble hallway, the clicking of her heels echoing to remind her she was practically alone in the building, Felicia wondered if she had been summoned into the office for something other than the Sterling merger. Was Clayton about to make a move? Her stomach churned with a mix of apprehension and excitement when she walked into the office.

It was immediately clear she had been called under false pretenses, but not for the passionate reason she'd hoped. George was an imposing figure, even in the wheelchair, framed as he was by the late afternoon light spilling in through the office's sole window. "Miss Calder."

She frowned. "What's going on? Why are you here?"

"I'm here to get rid of a problem—you."

Chapter Two

FELICIA TOOK A STEP back without thought when George maneuvered the chair toward her. She wasn't afraid of him, she assured herself. He was simply an annoyance to be dealt with. There was nothing the old man could do to her to force her to leave Clayton.

She couldn't help wondering why he looked so smug even as she continued telling herself she had nothing to fear. "I should call Clayton."

"Stop." His imperious command halted her in the process of reaching for her cell phone. His shaggy brows drew together low over his eyes, and his fierce frown made her tremble slightly despite herself. "You will leave Clayton out of this."

"I think you're the one who should stay out of the situation," she said, striving for a gentle tone. "I understand you're concerned for Clayton and your company, but I mean no harm to either of them."

George snorted. "Just as Trivanni came to no harm?"

Felicia's eyes widened. "What did you say?" she asked through trembling lips.

"I know all about you, Miss Calder. I know you come from nothing, and you are nothing. I am aware of your history of relationships with your former bosses, and by god, I shall not let Clayton end up the same way as your last conquest."

Feeling faint at the mention of Marco Trivanni, she swayed. To prevent falling, she placed a hand against the wall to brace herself. "I didn't do anything to Marco."

"I doubt his wife would agree with you, Miss Calder—or his doctors, for that matter."

She extended her other hand toward him. "Please let me explain. You have to understand."

He waved a large hand. "I know all I need to. It comes down to you not being fit to work for this company, let alone more intimately involved with a Witherspoon. You're going to resign tonight."

Somehow, she summoned the strength to stand upright and stop using the wall for support. "I did nothing wrong, and Clayton will believe me." She spoke with conviction.

"Your bank account tells a different story. The sum deposited five months ago looks like hush money to me."

"Severance," she said in a level voice, though a twinge of guilt assailed her. There was more to it than that, but George didn't want to hear her side of the story. Nothing she could say would change his opinion of her.

"Is that what they call it? Don't worry, Miss Calder. You will receive ample severance just for walking away." He named a figure so large it made her gasp. As he spoke, George was reaching into his jacket for his checkbook.

Her first instinct was to storm from the office. She hadn't been so insulted in her life, and she intended to tell George just what she thought of him and his offer as soon as her anger abated long enough to speak.

Her tongue broke its paralysis, but she hesitated. An image of Tanja flashed behind her eyes. Her sister navigating the streets of New York with a white cane, at the mercy of any number of things she couldn't control. Just a year ago, Tanja had been a happy, normal nineteen-year-old, until the headaches and loss of night vision, followed by the rapid onset of total blindness. Sitting before her was the answer to restoring her sister's sight.

George's pen hovered over the check. "Well, do we have a deal, Miss Calder?"

"No." Her voice was little more than a whisper. "I want twice that." It left a bitter taste in her mouth to form the words, but she tried to suppress her outraged pride and think logically. No matter how loathsome George's attitude and offer, she owed it to her sister to do everything she could to restore her sight. She had taken care of Tanja for years, and now wasn't the time to stop. She would do anything to get her sister into the program in Boston, regardless of what it did to her pride or self-esteem.

He barely batted an eyelash. "Of course." With a flourish, he filled in the blanks and ripped off the check. He waved it at her, and Felicia forced herself to walk forward to take it from his outstretched hand. Her stomach cramped when she held the slip of paper in her hand, and her vision blurred when he said, "Everyone has a price, Miss Calder. Yours was cheap, just like you."

"I'll tender my resignation tomorrow." She turned away from the nasty old man to keep him from seeing her tears.

"Tonight," he said firmly. "Once it's on Clayton's desk, I will personally see you to the airport."

She whirled around. "What?"

"I just bought something from you, Miss Calder. Your absence. You will be leaving the city tonight." He glowered up at her. "I want no opportunity for Clayton to see you again, to have you conveniently change your mind as soon as the check clears."

What did it matter where she was? Whether in New York or Ghana, Clayton would hate her if he ever learned she had accepted money to resign. She had no doubt George would tell him if she didn't leave. As vindictive as the man was, he would probably tell Clayton anyway. Once he knew the truth, she didn't want to be anywhere near him. It would be too humiliating to have to face him again.

"Fine, but I can find my own way."

"I said—"

She cut him off. "I have business to take care of first, but I guarantee you I'll be out of New York by tomorrow." With any luck, she and Tanja could get a flight to Boston later that night.

He seemed on the verge of arguing, but settled into silence. His eyes never left her as Tanja went to her desk to turn on her computer. When the word processing program loaded, she typed a brief letter of resignation, giving no reason for her abrupt departure. She feared Clayton would think the worst, maybe worry about her, but knew George would soon enlighten him to the truth of the situation.

The printer spat out the page quickly, and Felicia signed her name before she could have second thoughts. The check she had slipped into her pocket seemed hot, burning through her clothes, and nausea nearly overwhelmed her when she laid aside the pen and rose to her feet.

She left the letter centered on the desk, along with her nameplate and a small potted plant. She didn't worry about retrieving sundry items she had brought in when first hired. With a twinge of sadness, Felicia picked up the silver-framed photo on the edge of her desk, looking down at her sister's countenance. The two of them looked happy in the picture taken on the Santa Monica pier, and they had been. She remembered that day, how carefree they had been just weeks before their parents would be taken from them, and all innocent joy would be lost forever.

Felicia didn't look at George as she took her final walk across the office. When he started to speak, she held up her hand. "Save it. I have no more patience for your senseless hatred, old man." It gave her a tiny spark of pleasure to speak her mind, but it was the only bright spot of the day, aside from knowing she could finally offer her sister hope again.

***

"BUT HOW?" TANJA ASKED for at least the tenth time in twenty minutes.

Felicia bit back an impatient sigh. "Don't worry about that right now. Just concentrate on getting yourself ready. Our flight leaves tomorrow morning at nine-thirty, and the clinic is expecting you at one o'clock."

"I can't go. My classes...my part-time job..."

"The university will still be there when you're finished with treatment, if you still need to go there. Don't worry about working. I have enough to cover our expenses for a while."

Tanja sounded upset. "I'm not sure about this."

"Why are you hesitating?" She winced at the sharpness of her words and softened her tone. "This is your only chance to ever see again, kiddo."

"I know, but I'm scared. It's so risky, and the results are mixed."

She sighed impatiently. "It will be worth it when you're back to normal again. Please don't worry so. I've always taken care of you, haven't I?"

"Yes."

She would bet Tanja was chewing on her lower lip right then, though she couldn't see her through the phone. "Trust me. Focus on getting your sight back, and let me worry about everything else."

After another hesitation, the other woman sighed. "All right. I'll be ready. When will you pick me up?"

"I'll come for you around seven. We can—" She broke off when her doorbell rang, followed almost immediately by a loud pounding. Her mouth went dry, and she barely managed to hide her apprehension when she spoke again. "I'll call you back later. There's someone at the door."

She hung up the cordless and tossed it on the sofa as the knocking became more insistent. Instinct urged her not to open the door, and she hesitated with her hand on the chain, unable to summon the courage to even peek through the peephole. She already knew who her visitor was and why he was there. He knew. She didn't know how, but he must, and she couldn't face him.

"Open the door this minute, Felicia. I know you're home. Your doorman said you haven't been out all evening."

His anger was palpable through the wood separating them, and she shivered under the force of it. "Please go away, Clayton. I'm busy."

"I'll bet. Open the door, or I'll call the police."

19

She frowned. "I think you're confused. Shouldn't I be the one calling the police if you don't leave?"

"Feel free, but you'll end up in jail right beside me. Extortion is a felony, you know."

His threat sounded serious, and she swallowed the lump in her throat as she opened the door, leaving on the security chain. She winced at the rage in his expression, and her knees trembled. "Please go away," she said in a weak whisper.

"Let me in."

Felicia shook her head. "We have nothing to say to each other."

Clayton lunged forward, his face inches from hers. With gritted teeth, he said, "I have plenty to say to you. It's your choice whether your neighbors hear it too. If you don't want a scene, unchain the door and let me in. Now!"

She closed the door in a hurry, confident he would withdraw his face in time. It was tempting to turn the deadbolt again, instead of releasing the security chain, but she had to face him. Somehow, it would be easier if she wasn't wearing a silky red robe she'd slipped on for comfort. And nothing else.

He barged in as soon as the chain rattled against the door, not even waiting for her to open it again. Clayton slammed the door behind him, never taking his gaze from her. She stared at him anxiously, wondering what he would do next. "What are you doing here, Clayton?"

"I went into the office to work on the Sterling merger. There's still a lot left to accomplish before we officially take them over." His disheveled state indicated he had been working hard. His tie was crooked, and he had discarded his jacket somewhere.

She had never seen him in anything except a suit, so the crisp whiteness of his shirt was enough to make her mouth water, even under the circumstances. It set off his tan and emphasized the darkness of his short hair and eyes.

Felicia blinked, trying to tear her attention from his body. She nodded, daring to hope he was here for something business-related. "I left a stack of memos on your desk before leaving." Maybe he hadn't seen the letter of resignation on her desk. Perhaps his anger was due to a hitch with the deal.

He disabused her of that hope quickly. "Which time before leaving, Felicia? Your letter stunned me. Not a word of explanation, not even anything remotely personal." His eyes, already dark with anger, seemed to burn blacker still. "You thanked me for the opportunity to work with me and said you had to resign. Don't you think you owed me an explanation?"

She swallowed down moisture at the back of her throat. "It's a family situation."

"Don't lie to me anymore. You've lied enough already."

Her eyes widened. "When have I ever lied to you before?"

The words were more of a growl than a statement. "When you submitted your résumé, for one. You told me you'd taken time off to reevaluate your career. I guess you were afraid I wouldn't hire you if you admitted the truth about your last place of employment."

She sagged forward. Why hadn't she anticipated George telling Clayton everything? It had been the old man's goal to alienate her from Clayton, and what better way than his twisted version of what had happened with Marco Trivanni? "I can explain."

"I don't care." A vein bulged in his forehead. "It doesn't matter. None of it matters anymore."

The finality of his words suggested he was on the verge of leaving, and she battled a surge of relief mixed with sadness. This wasn't how she had wanted things to end between them.

She squared her shoulders. "If that's all then, I have business to attend to." She still had arrangements to make for their stay in Boston and was awaiting a fax from the assistant of the director of the clinic with further information about the study in which Tanja was enrolling. After all that, she hoped to have time for a good cry.

"That's not all," he said silkily. "I'm not through with you yet."

"What do you want from me?" she asked through trembling lips.

"What I paid for."

Her confusion must have shown, because he expounded. "When I saw the letter, I knew my father had something to do with your abrupt resignation." He shook his head. "Can you believe I actually feared for your safety? I thought he might have harmed you. I didn't see how else he could have persuaded you to leave me, not when we were getting so close."

She closed her eyes as each word speared her heart like a dart. "Please..."

He ignored her interruption. "I didn't believe him at first. I was certain he was lying. You aren't the kind of person he described. You would never lie to me about your past. You certainly couldn't have driven a married man to attempted suicide after your affair went sour. You absolutely wouldn't allow my father to buy you off—not only that, but threatened him with sexual harassment charges if he didn't meet your price." A harsh laugh, holding little amusement, escaped him. "I was wrong about you, wasn't I?"

"I didn't—" She broke off, knowing he wouldn't believe her assertion she hadn't threatened George, especially since she couldn't deny his other charges. Numbness settled over her at the crushing weight of disappointment reflected from his eyes. "I'm sorry if I hurt you."

He blinked, and any trace of vulnerability disappeared. "I'm not hurt, Felicia. I'm not even angry now." His body language belied that statement. "In fact, I'm grateful to my father for showing me just what kind of person you are. I have no reason to feel guilty for what I'm doing."

"What's that?" she asked warily.

"Claiming what I bought." He scowled. "Father wasn't happy about me reimbursing him the cost of your cooperation, but didn't keep protesting when I threatened to have him removed from the board. He knows I can do it, so he fell in line." Clayton reached out to take hold of her upper arms, drawing her closer. "I own you now."

Felicia shook her head. "You can't own someone else."

"The check I wrote to my father says otherwise."

She bit her lip, frantically trying to decide on a course of action. She would have to return the check. He couldn't threaten her with extortion if she didn't cash it. But she couldn't return it. After what she'd gone through to acquire the money, she couldn't just hand it over, leaving Clayton with a horrible opinion of her and no job. It seemed unlikely he or George could prove extortion anyway, based simply on the old man's claim she had tried to blackmail him with the threat of sexual harassment. She still didn't have the time or money to fight the claim right now if she wanted Tanja to get her sight back.

He seemed to read her mind. "Don't bother returning the money. You're well worth the price of acquisition...or you will be."

Fear dried her mouth, making it difficult to respond. "What do you expect from me?"

"For one thing, I want you back in the office tomorrow morning. I can't spare you right now until the merger goes through. After that, you'll need to train your replacement."

Relief swept through her. "Of course. I'll pay back whatever else I owe you after my employment ends."

He quirked a brow. "I'm not finished. Did you think I would let you off so easily?"

She shook her head. "I can explain why I accepted your father's offer. I can explain everything."

He held up a hand. "As I said, I don't care to hear rationalizations for your greed. All I want from you is what I paid for—your body."

23

Her eyes widened when he pulled her against him. She couldn't believe it was happening, that he was about to kiss her, even as her body melted against his firmly muscled frame. Of its own volition, her head tipped back and she moistened her lips as he brought his mouth against hers. His lips were firm and demanding, molding hers to his possession. Felicia groaned when he buried a hand in her hair to pull her neck back even more, allowing his tongue to penetrate her mouth.

She wrapped her arms around his neck, anxious to be closer to Clayton. It didn't matter how they had come to this right then. She only cared about tasting him. With eager strokes, she met each thrust of his tongue, savoring the trace of brandy she detected. Pressing herself closer, Felicia brought her hands to his shoulders, then lower, to his chest. His muscles rippled under her hands as she pressed her palms against the silky cotton of his dress shirt and the heat of his skin scorched her palms.

Clayton seemed intent on devouring her. His tongue had swept every inch of her mouth several times over and he began thrusting it in and out suggestively, in time with his hips as he pumped them. Felicia wanted to be closer to him still, but couldn't. They were pressed against each other so tightly only their clothing served as a barrier to separate them.

He stroked his tongue across her lips before moving his mouth, brushing his lips against her cheek on his way to her ear. Felicia cried out when he nipped her earlobe before whispering, "Felicia." The way he said her name was almost as pleasurable as his tongue tracing the contour of her ear before he sucked the lobe into his mouth once again.

Her hands shook as she tugged impatiently at the hem of his shirt to remove it from the waistband of his pants. It took more concentration than it should have to work the small buttons through the buttonholes and she whimpered with need when she managed to push open the shirt to reveal his bare chest. "Clayton." His name was more a cry of passion than an actual sound as she placed her palms against the lightly haired skin. He retaliated by bringing his mouth to the bend of her shoulder, to suck on her neck. Her insides warmed and melted, making it difficult to do anything besides enjoy his touch.

A deep-throated groan left Clayton when she raked her nails lightly across his nipples, propelling her to repeat the action. His throaty sound of satisfaction fed her own and she ignored the voice in the back of her mind trying to get her attention. She didn't care about common sense at the moment.

Clayton made short work of the robe, while she tried focusing on removing his belt. Her persistence paid off, as did his, and they were soon standing together in the living room, bare body to bare body, his paler skin a beautiful contrast to her darker shade. The hair on his chest tickled her nipples, and she squirmed with pleasure.

He brought his mouth to hers again, his lips taking possession of hers. Felicia swept her tongue inside the moist confines of his before he could edge inside hers, taking control. Her moans of pleasure mirrored his as she absorbed his taste.

She cried out his name when he cupped her breasts, his thumbs rubbing against the firm buds of her nipples with confident strokes. "Clayton," she whispered, dropping her face to his chest and burrowing against him. His name was her talisman, the only thing keeping her anchored to the world, and she found herself almost screaming it when he lifted her higher. Instinctively her thighs locked around his waist as he entered her for the first time.

He filled her completely—almost to the point of too much—and she clutched his back to keep her balance. Her nails dug into his skin when Clayton began thrusting. He supported her with his hands cupping her bottom, bringing her tightly against him with each thrust. "That's amazing, Clayton." That she could manage any coherent sound surprised her.

He buried his head in her thick mane of still-frizzed tresses. "So perfect."

Convulsions deep inside her womb instigated an orgasm and she shuddered, tightening around him. He convulsed inside her, and they fell backward together on the sofa. Felicia struggled to catch her breath, still ravaged by the force of their passions and her earth-shattering release. It had been unforgettable, more than she could have imagined in her most erotic fantasies. So why did she still feel empty?

"Worth every penny," he said in a different tone—a mix of smugness and smoldering anger. "I've imagined you like this, but didn't want to rush you. You seemed so sweet and a bit uncertain." He sneered. "Now, I don't have to worry about building trust just to get you in my bed."

She jumped away from him as though burned. Memory came crashing back, and she cupped her hand over her mouth to keep from crying out. How could she have been so stupid? He hadn't taken her because he wanted her, but because he thought he was entitled to do so.

Her mouth firmed, and she glared at him. "I hope you enjoyed it, because it will never happen again."

He stared up at her impassively, seemingly unbothered by their state of undress, and showing no sign of leaving. "Wrong. It will happen when and where I want it to."

"Because you own me?" Her voice was full of anger, but she didn't miss the shaky note underlying it. Felicia hoped he didn't notice the hurt in her tone or expression.

He smiled, a sexy quirking of just one side of his mouth. "Partly, but mostly because you want it to happen too."

She sagged, unable to deny his assertion. How could she resist him when she wanted him so desperately? Making love with him once hadn't sated her. It had only deepened her hunger for Clayton, regardless of what he thought of her.

She hugged herself, both in an attempt to hide her breasts and to disguise her conflict. "Will you leave now? I'm tired."

In an infuriating fashion, Clayton shook his head. "I'm not going anywhere, Felicia."

Her eyes widened and she shook her head. "You have to. I have things to do."

"You have nothing to do other than spend the night in bed with me."

"You don't understand—"

Clayton gained his feet in one fluid motion, a visual performance that took her breath away as she watched the coordinated way his muscles flexed and contracted under his skin, reminding her just how it felt to be joined with him.

He walked toward her slowly, as if he had all night. "I'm not letting you out of my sight. I don't trust you not to run."

"I won't..." She trailed off, remembering the forthcoming trip. "I mean, I have to go somewhere, but I'll pay you back when I return."

He tucked a long strand of hair behind her ear. "Yes, you will. You've made a start, and now it's time to continue." In seconds, he had lifted her into his arms and was headed down the hallway, seeming to know exactly where her bedroom was. "I'm going to spend the night getting to know every inch of you."

He seemed to swallow all the space in her bedroom, making it difficult to breathe as he lowered her to the bed. The feminine pastels should have been a jarring backdrop for his masculinity, but he looked right, settled on her bed, against her pale pink sheets. Maybe it was because she had imagined him there so many times in the past few months.

As he straddled her, she put up her hands, resting them against her chest. "You don't have to do this. Please, let me explain."

He sighed, sounding impatient. "Enough. I can think of much more pleasurable uses for your mouth."

She moaned, unable to resist picturing the mental image his words evoked.

Clayton chuckled while shifting his weight to free one of his hands. Felicia tensed when he brought a hand between her thighs, his fingers slipping inside her folds to find the slippery little bud hiding within. She cried out as he stroked her clit, arching against his hand.

"So hot, sweetness." Clayton penetrated her with two of his fingers. "And so tight. Surprising, considering your previous...experience."

She flinched, torn between anger and hurt, all the while under the onslaught of his expert fingers. Pride demanded she push him away. Felicia pressed her palms against his chest. "Get off me."

"Not yet." With ruthless precision, Clayton continued stroking and thrusting his fingers inside her.

Tears of shame blurred her eyes as her body responded, giving him the climax he sought. She turned her head, trying to hide her tears as they escaped to trickle down her cheeks.

Clayton said something in Italian that sounded like a curse. With the same hand he'd had between her legs, he wiped away the moisture with his thumb. "I apologize. That comment was unnecessary."

She took a deep breath, struggling to restore her calm before speaking. Her voice was still thick with tears when she said, "This isn't going to work. You hate me. How can you still want me?"

Clayton eased himself off her body to lie beside her. "I don't hate you. I wish I could, but I don't. I don't understand the avarice that drives you, but I had a privileged upbringing that you lacked."

She didn't try to offer an explanation again. "I can't do this. Your snide words...the anger. I just can't." But what choice was there? Even if she could convince him to accept the check from George and release her from this twisted deal, Tanja would be just as blind, with no hope.

Clayton caressed her hip. "I can't promise I'll always be able to control my anger with you, but I will not make such comments again, especially when we're in bed together."

In defeat, she rolled into his arms as he turned her. The thought of being his whore for however long he wanted her was heartbreaking, but Tanja's needs came before her own. Not that her needs didn't include Clayton, at least physically, she admitted to herself when he entered her.

It would be even more humiliating for him to know the depth of her desire.

Silently, she counseled herself not to reveal that she still planned to leave tomorrow. He would be furious, but Tanja needed her. When she returned, she would make herself available until his need for revenge burned itself out. Perhaps he would even reconsider the whole idea during her absence, since he'd now had sex with her. She allowed herself to cling to the hope as Clayton drove in and out of her, hoping each thrust brought her one step closer to absolution.

Chapter Three

HE'D BEEN TRUE TO HIS word, having spent most of the night taking her in myriad ways. Felicia was sore in places she hadn't even remembered existed, and the hot water cascading over her did little to ease the pleasurable aches. It would serve him right if every muscle in his body screamed in protest from their night of sex, though he had seemed disgustingly chipper upon waking. She needed coffee before she could even consider being half that alert.

She had to admit the previous night had served to invigorate rather than exhaust her as she might have expected. It had been too long since her last lover to remember if she had always felt this way after a night of vigorous sex. Being unable to remember her morning-after reactions with previous partners spoke for itself. Clayton was different, and being with him was unlike anything she had ever experienced.

It was going to be hard to leave him, but she had no choice. Tanja needed her, but she couldn't have stayed anyway, not under the circumstances. She had come to that realization sometime around dawn. Her heart was already at risk, but there was no way he would ever love her after she had taken money to get out of his life. Staying with Clayton would destroy her. Felicia knew she would have to return to serve her sentence in his bed, but she needed to figure out a way to protect her heart first.

After stripping off the shower cap, she dried off and dressed quickly, not from eagerness to face Clayton, but because time was growing short. Wasting precious time she didn't have trying to tame her hair quickly, when she needed a lot more time to make it look decent, she finally gave up and shoved it all into a messy bun. She had to get rid of him so she could pick up Tanja in time for their flight.

He had made himself at home in the kitchen, evidenced by the stack of pancakes and orange juice on the table. He sat at the table, talking on his cell phone, but looked up when she walked in. He held up a finger and spent another moment on the phone before closing it.

"It's getting late," she said as soon as he hung up.

"Yes." Clayton pushed away from the table and stood up. "I have to leave now."

Relief swept through her, but she tried not to show it. "Really?"

"My father is pitching a fit and insisting his assistant contacts the board to arrange an emergency meeting."

She lifted a brow. "Because of...this?" she asked with a wave of her hand to indicate the two of them.

He shrugged. "Probably, but I'll take care of it. He's upset things didn't go his way, but as soon as I point out how his trying to remove me as CEO will undermine the merger he so desperately wants, I think he'll let it drop."

Felicia disdained the orange juice in favor of a mug of coffee from the pot. She had forgotten to turn on the timer last night, so he must have brewed a pot, though he rarely drank coffee. His thoughtfulness caused tears to prick the back of her eyes, and she cleared her throat, impatient with the emotions assailing her. "I'm sure you'll deal with it."

"Of course." He drained his orange juice in a long swallow and brought the glass to the dishwasher. "Hold down the fort until I make it into the office. I'm confident you can deal with anything that might arise."

"You still trust me?"

"Not at all, but I know you can handle my business. You've always been good at that." He ignored her attempt to recoil when he pressed a kiss against her mouth. "I'll see you soon."

Felicia managed a nod, holding herself stiffly until he left the kitchen. She didn't relax her posture until the front door closed a couple of minutes later. As soon as he was gone, she set the mug of coffee on the counter and raced down the hall to her bedroom. She hadn't even started packing before his arrival last night, so she retrieved a suitcase from the closet and tossed items inside haphazardly. She could acquire anything she neglected to bring with her in Boston.

Felicia called for an Uber with the app on her cellphone as she rushed down to meet it. The driver was prompt and arrived five minutes later, but she jumped out almost as soon as she'd slid inside the vehicle. Then, cursing all the way, she rushed back to her apartment for the paperwork faxed to her by the clinic.

Things went more smoothly after that, with Tanja waiting for her on the corner, suitcase in tow. They cleared security at the airport in record time, and their plane took off only two minutes late. Felicia wanted to think everything would be okay, but it all seemed to be going too well. Still, she released tension she hadn't been aware of maintaining once the plane left the tarmac and New York fell rapidly away.

Putting distance between herself and Clayton was the right thing to do. Perspective would give her time to come up with a solution to the mess in which she found herself and would give Clayton time to realize he couldn't treat her as his sex toy. Once his initial anger had time to dissipate, they could work out a civilized repayment plan. Maybe. Even if he wouldn't be reasonable, she would just have to refuse to let him use her body for revenge.

Not that she'd been very good at telling him no, she acknowledged wryly. She was buying herself time to put up a wall between herself and Clayton. By the time the plane touched down at Logan, she almost had herself convinced she could see Clayton again and not fall into bed with him.

CLAYTON ENTERED THE elevator for his office feeling surprisingly good in spite of what had happened with Felicia. Well, probably because of what had happened with her, but not what had led to last night. He'd dealt with his father and was now on his way to work. To see her, his lover.

It was ridiculous to feel so excited to see her again, especially knowing what he did about her. Only a fool let himself fall for someone who was greedy and scheming. He tried to understand how she could put money above their burgeoning relationship. As he'd told her, he couldn't relate to that kind of need, having grown up in a wealthy family. Still, he couldn't imagine any circumstances that would have made him take money to leave her if the situation had been reversed.

He had to keep it firmly in mind why she was now his lover. In effect, he had bought her, as distasteful as that was. It wasn't the best way to deal with her betrayal, but he didn't have it in him to overlook her actions, or to just let her go. Fool that he was, he cared too much... Clayton squashed that thought as it formed. All he needed from her was physical pleasure until he no longer wanted her. Any feelings he'd had for Felicia before she'd revealed her true nature had to die a quick death.

Mentally steeling himself for the assault to his senses the moment he saw her, he entered the office. Immediately, he noticed her desk was empty. As he drew nearer, he saw it was exactly as he had left it last night. Feeling just a spark of hope that he was misinterpreting the scene, he knocked on the office washroom. When no one answered, he tried the door, finding it unlocked, and pushed it open. It was as empty as the office.

Anger exploded through him, and he cursed as he stomped back to her desk. Her home computer was connected to the office's network, so she could work from home. It took Clayton very little time to call up her internet history, to get an idea of where she had gone. Rage made his hands shake, and he refused to recognize the hurt rushing through him at her betrayal.

"ARE YOU SURE YOU DON'T want me to stay?" Felicia asked Tanja several hours later.

Her sister nodded. "Yeah, I'm sure. I have a lot of tests ahead of me, and you can't accompany me. Why should you hang out in the hospital room when you could be resting? You look exhausted."

Felicia eyed the patient suite where the staff had installed Tanja. "This place is probably nicer than my room."

"Go." Tanja tossed a pillow in her general vicinity. "Get some fresh air and see the sights. We haven't been to Boston since we were little."

Felicia blinked. "You're right. I'd forgotten we came here with Mom and Dad."

"I was seven, so you must have been about thirteen."

Tanja had spoken without much emotion, but Felicia couldn't expect her sister to go to pieces at the memories of the long-ago family vacation when she herself had forgotten all about it. There were more pressing matters on which to dwell, instead of bittersweet memories. "I might sightsee later, but right now I'm going to sleep." She stifled a yawn. "I am pretty tired."

"You must have had a late night." Tanja grinned. "Up all night with your boss?"

"I had a lot of work to get through." She spoke more sharply than she'd intended. Before last night, she would have laughed with her sister, but was too sensitive to make light of it right then, though Tanja had no idea her teasing had been spot-on the truth. Seeing her sister flinch, she softened her tone. "Sorry. I'm just tired."

Tanja lifted one shoulder. "It's okay. Just get some rest."

Reluctantly, Felicia got out of the sumptuous easy chair and walked over to where her sister sat on the queen-size bed. She bent to hug her. "I feel bad leaving you here alone, kiddo."

"I'll be fine," said Tanja with barely a tremor in her voice. "It's just some tests, and I've been through most of them before with Dr. Batts."

After a second hug, she stood up. "I'll be back to have dinner with you."

"How about breakfast? I'm probably going to be pretty tired after all the poking and prodding."

She nodded out of habit before remembering Tanja couldn't see the motion. "If that's what you want. I'll come back in the morning. You want me to bring you anything?"

"Are you kidding? Have you seen the menu? I was reading through it while you completed the paperwork. It's a feast."

"How did you...?"

"Braille," Tanja said quickly. "Everything is in Braille too." A frown distorted her delicate features. "Makes me wonder what kind of success rate they have, if their facilities are so blind-friendly."

"They have to accommodate everyone." She cleared her throat, trying to sound cheerful when she spoke again. "It's all going to be fine. I promise."

Something that might have passed for a smile crossed her sister's face. "I know. Now scoot."

Felicia grasped her suitcase and left her sister's room. The hallway was as opulent as the rest of the facility thus far, making her wonder how much of the exorbitant fee she had paid to get Tanja in went to research, and how much went to maintenance of the surroundings. What did it matter? She would pay twice as much, and gladly, to have Tanja's sight restored.

She had deliberately booked lodging within walking distance of the clinic, but the case was weighing heavily by the time she walked the three blocks and found the charming bed and breakfast she had selected. Since their stay could be a long one, she had chosen a place that would be more like home than a chain hotel. If they were going to be there for months, she would see about renting an apartment. In the meantime, Herringbone House would do.

Mrs. Herringbone herself manned the desk, according to the nameplate. She was in her mid-sixties, pleasantly plump, with an infectious smile. As soon as she heard Felicia's name, her smile widened further. "Of course, dear. I have your room all ready." She came out from behind the desk and took the case from Felicia before she could protest. "Let's get you settled."

"But...don't I need to register?"

"No need, dear. Your husband saw to all that already."

Felicia swayed. "My what?"

A frown furrowed the old woman's face. "Your husband arrived a couple of hours ago. He upgraded your room to the honeymoon suite." She chuckled.

"Oh." Numbly, Felicia followed Mrs. Herringbone up the stairs, idly noting the intricate details on the railing and each balustrade. "I see."

"I was sorry to hear your plans had changed though."

"Hmm, yeah."

Mrs. Herringbone shook her head. "I love it when my guests stay with me a while, giving me a chance to get to know them. It's a shame you're checking out tomorrow."

Felicia's lips tightened. "He—my husband—told you that?"

The older woman nodded, apparently oblivious to her outrage. "He looks like he works too hard, dear. It's a shame his business is interfering with your vacation."

"Yes, it is." She was seething with anger by the time Mrs. Herringbone brought her to a room at the end of the hall on the second landing.

She handed Felicia an old-fashioned key, patting her hand in the process. "Enjoy your time together, dear. If you want me to send up a supper tray, just ring the desk."

"Thanks." Felicia managed a smile that disappeared the minute Mrs. Herringbone was gone. She unlocked the door briskly, preparing herself for a confrontation with Clayton. How dare he be so highhanded?

Anger carried her across the threshold in seconds, and she slammed the door behind her, gaining some satisfaction from the way it made Clayton jump. "How dare you?"

Her anger faltered when he strode toward her, dying in the face of his. Gone was the cheerful man from this morning, or even the bossy, but tender lover from last night. Here stood a reincarnation of the angry man who had entered her apartment yesterday, except his anger had clearly intensified.

"How dare you?" he countered. "The minute I turned my back, you ran." Clayton shook his head. "I can't believe I was so stupid as to trust you, even a little."

"Wait." She backed away as he continued to bear down on her. "I told you I had to go somewhere."

"I thought you understood our agreement, Felicia. Your body for a large sum of money." He lifted a brow. "Or did you lie to me about accepting our deal too?"

She shook her head. "Of course not. If you'd just listen—"

"I've heard enough lies come out of your beautiful, deceitful mouth," he said so sarcastically she winced. "I wouldn't believe a thing you said unless God himself vouched for you."

Felicia hung her head, not sure how to handle his anger. Even last night, he hadn't been this cold with her. Any chance she'd had of reasoning with him, or explaining her actions, had clearly died in the wake of what he viewed as her flight from him. "What are you going to do to me?"

"Tomorrow, we're going back to New York, where I'm watching your every move." He followed her as she backed away, until she was pressed against the wall. Clayton pressed his body against hers. "I'm going to keep you in my sight until I decide I've gotten my money's worth."

"I can't." She tried to resist when he grasped her wrists and brought them over her head, but part of her didn't want to. That part of Felicia just wanted to throw herself into his arms and beg forgiveness for her perceived sins.

"Wrong answer." His tone could have frozen water, and his unyielding expression granted no mercy as he pinned her hands above her head, holding them in place with one hand. His other hand roamed freely under her jacket, seeking out one of her breasts. He tugged hard on her nipple, making her gasp, but with pleasure instead of pain. Her flimsy plan of refusing to allow him access to her body died.

He moved quickly, stripping her with a single-minded determination that compensated for him using only one hand. Felicia knew she should resist, but her body called out for his possession, even as her mind cringed away from her own actions. How could she so wantonly abandon herself to Clayton, allowing him to use her?

The ability to think left her when Clayton had her stripped bare. He released his hold on her wrists, and she started to lower her arms. "Leave them," he said harshly, making her freeze.

Her mouth went dry when Clayton disrobed, seeming to remove his clothes at a pace designed to drive her insane. She moved one hand toward him, eager to assist, and he stopped. Clayton grasped the offending limb and brought it back above her head again. "Don't move."

"Please."

He was clearly delighting in her agony as he finally undressed completely, slipped on a condom, and stepped closer. He hovered just out of range, so she couldn't feel his body against hers, just the almost-touch of his skin near hers. "Who do you belong to, Felicia?"

She shook her head, refusing to give him the answer he sought, to debase herself to that extent. She closed her eyes, biting down hard on her lip when he fondled one of her breasts, his thumb gently stroking her nipple.

"Who, Felicia?"

Once again, she shook her head, though more feebly. Her strength to resist him was rapidly diminishing. When he dipped his head to take her nut-brown nipple into his mouth, she cried out.

"Say it, Felicia."

Did he have to keep saying her name like that, with that sexy drawl, prolonging each syllable until she thought she might go mad? "No," she whispered.

He held his body so close to hers she could feel the hair on his chest tickling her nipples. "You know you belong to me. Surrender." Clayton took her hands, grasping one in each of his and bracing them against the wall. She tossed her head, finding her resistance worn away. "Mine, Felicia. Confirm it, and I'll give you what you want."

She dropped her head, giving in. "I'm yours."

"For as long as I want you," he prompted.

Tears blurred her vision, and she managed to nod. Her humiliation was total, but she wondered what else he had in store for her.

To her surprise, Clayton's mouth moved to the bend of her neck, forcing her to straighten it. She moaned when he stroked the sensitive flesh with his tongue, and he took advantage of the moment to lift his head and seize her mouth.

She expected him to ravage her, to mark her as his possession, but his lips were gentle on hers, a marked contrast to the hardness of his body as he let himself melt against her. His tongue penetrated her lips as his cock entered her, and Felicia responded with passionate abandon, thrusting against him ardently as she returned his kisses. His grip on her hands had loosened from a hold of confinement to one of connection, and she squeezed her fingers around his hand. Clayton's hips formed a natural rest for her thighs when she locked them around him as he plunged deep inside her, making her breathless with need and pleasure.

They came together, a chorus of grunts and groans voicing their release. Felicia laid her head against his shoulder, licking the skin and finding it tangy with the salt of his perspiration. She didn't have words to describe the experience, to do justice to how good it had been, and words wouldn't have been appropriate anyway. The peace between them was too fragile to shatter right then.

He eased away from the wall, bringing her with him. Still, they didn't speak. As he lowered her to the Victorian bed, he gently kissed each of her closed eyelids. Only after he had joined her, wrapping his arms around her, did he finally speak. "Rest, sweetness. Tomorrow will be a long day."

FELICIA LIFTED THE phone to call Tanja after consulting the card that had her sister's room and phone number printed on it. Reluctantly, she pressed the keys, seeing no other way around things. Clayton had demanded that she return with him to New York. She doubted her ability to make him believe she'd had good reason for taking the money. It pained her, but her own guilty conscience prodded her to give Clayton whatever he wanted. Tanja probably wouldn't understand, but that couldn't be helped. She wouldn't be any more useful to her sister here than she would be in New York City if her thoughts stayed centered around Clayton, and how she had hurt him.

Her sister answered on the second ring, sounding tired. "Hello."

"Hi, Tanja."

"Felicia." Her voice brightened considerably. "You'd better be calling to tell me you're on your way. I'm starving."

She sighed. "Sorry, but no. I can't make breakfast."

"Oh. What's up?"

"I have to go back to New York."

Tanja made an ambiguous sound. "Are you serious?"

"I'm sorry, kiddo, but I have no choice." That was an understatement. "Do you want to come home and return later for treatment?"

After a hesitation, Tanja said, "That doesn't make sense. I just don't know if I can do this alone." She sounded on the verge of tears.

Felicia's stomach cramped in reaction. "I have faith in you, Tanja. You're going to do just fine." She forced herself to sound cheerful. "You know I'll be back just as soon as I can."

"I know." She cleared her throat. "Maybe I'll be done with the program by the time you can get away from work again."

"Maybe." Just how long would Clayton expect her to play his revenge game? When would he decide she had paid him back sufficiently by using her body as payment?

"I love you, Felicia."

"I love you too." She set the phone back on the handset gently, her fingers lingering on the device for a moment, wishing she could take back the phone call she'd just made, along with the reason for having to make it.

As she turned, Felicia bumped into Clayton. Gasping with surprise, she clutched her chest. "You startled me."

"Sorry to interrupt such an intimate conversation." His eyes glowed darkly with anger.

"Clayton—"

"Get dressed. Our plane leaves soon." He turned his back on her, and his posture communicated he wasn't open to a discussion regarding what he thought he'd heard.

With a small shake of her head, she turned away from him. Futility weighed on her, making it almost impossible to summon the energy required to shower and dress. There was an irreparable breach between them now, and all the sex in the world wasn't going to heal it. Any hopes she'd had of a meaningful relationship had died the moment she'd accepted George's offer. Yet, what other choice could she have made? The worst part was Clayton would never know her reasons because he refused to hear them—not that he would believe anything she told him now.

An hour later, Felicia sat beside Clayton on his private jet, pretending to read a magazine she'd found on the table. He was absorbed in a stack of paperwork probably related to the Sterling merger. Other than the occasional brooding glance cast in her direction, he might as well have been set in stone.

Her fingers itched to reach for her cell phone to call Tanja, but she hesitated. Even if the call would go through, she didn't want to speak in front of Clayton. A part of her liked having him think there was another man in her life. It made her feel safe and protected to have a buffer between them, however flimsy. As long as an imaginary lover stood between them, he would maintain an emotional distance. It could be vital to her self-preservation and might be the only thing to keep her from doing something stupid, like falling in love with him.

He abruptly closed the file as they neared the private landing strip. "We'll go straight to your apartment."

She arched a brow. "I'm a little...sore from last night."

"So you can pack," he said in a cool tone.

Felicia frowned. "Pack? For what? Are we going on a business trip?"

Clayton opened his briefcase to place the file neatly inside. "You're moving in with me."

Her mouth dropped open and she closed it so quickly her teeth clicked together. "What? Are you crazy?"

"I'm not letting you out of my sight again." He looked up from the briefcase to watch her with narrowed eyes. "I don't trust you not to run off once more. You obviously have a lover in Boston. Who knows where else you might have men waiting for you?"

"I'm not a whore." She spoke loudly enough to worry the crew in the cockpit had heard her, even through the door separating it from the main cabin.

Clayton snorted. "What else do you call a woman who trades her body for money?" His cool façade cracked slightly, revealing a hint of anger and something more. "How many other men have you done this to, Felicia? Was Trivanni's family the first you extorted money from, or

43

just the latest?" He shook his head. "What drove you to behave like this?"

Anger warred with pain, eventually winning. She glared at him. "You've obviously already figured it all out. Why should I offer any explanations now?"

"Why indeed, when there can be no justification for your actions?"

"Precisely." She straightened her jacket. "I'm not moving in with you. You'll just have to trust me to keep up my end of the deal."

"But I don't trust you. You will be moving in with me because, as much as you hate to admit it, your body wants mine with a marked lack of reason." He seemed confident she would be taking up residence with him by the end of the day.

With a mutinous set of her mouth, she said, "I am not leaving my home. It will be a cold day in hell before I give up my autonomy to be at your beck and call."

Two hours later, Felicia followed Clayton into his sumptuous penthouse apartment in a twelve-story building in mid-town. A chill ran down her spine, making her wonder if hell had indeed frozen over.

Chapter Four

IT WAS STRANGE TO BE back at her desk less than twenty-four hours later, as if nothing had changed. Yet, everything had changed. She now knew Clayton as intimately as anyone could know another, but knew nothing about his heart. He had closed it to her.

The only thing she could take freely from him was his body, and while she enjoyed the sex, she wanted more. Once upon a time, she had dreamed of a relationship with Clayton that included making love. Now, they had a pale imitation of what might have been, built solely on lies, misconceptions, and sex. It was physically satisfying but left her emotionally bereft.

Her phone buzzed. "Did you find that file yet?" Clayton asked, sounding impatient.

She winced, realizing while lost in her reverie at least fifteen minutes had passed since he asked for some key paperwork that had been missing from the Sterling packet. "Just now. It was misfiled." Better to look incompetent than to appear weepy. It was bad enough she was emotionally vested in the travesty they were acting out. He didn't need to know she felt anything remotely sentimental.

As if the day wasn't already bad enough, the sound of George's wheelchair entering her office let her know it was about to get worse. She pretended not to see the old man as she lifted the folder and turned toward Clayton's office.

He dashed her hopes of avoiding a confrontation with his first spiteful statement. "Now you're his whore, aren't you?"

She took a deep breath and tried counting to ten. Before she even made it to five, he continued.

"It sickens me to know you're sharing his bed." A wheezing laugh escaped him. "However, I'm comforted to know the affair will be short-lived. I won't ever have to worry about him trying to marry you and have nappy-haired grandchildren running around now that he knows what you are."

Felicia whirled around, glaring down at him. "He knows what you are too—a manipulative, hateful old man, who will stop at nothing to control those around him." Somehow, she managed to steady her voice. "You might have opened his eyes to my so-called flaws, but at what cost to your relationship with him?"

George snorted. "As if a whore like you could come between my son and me. You're trash, pure and simple. Not a cent to your name that you've earned the old-fashioned way, no breeding of which to speak, and nothing to redeem you. I'd do what I did a thousand times over. My only regret is I didn't personally ensure you left New York as I had planned."

"You—" Whatever might have flown from her tongue halted with Clayton's arrival. He strode out of his office, glaring at both of them.

"Enough. I won't have you two behaving this way, especially not in the office." His disapproving gaze alternated between the two of them, making her feel like a recalcitrant child. "What if a client witnessed this display?"

She swallowed a ball of anger and managed a nod. "You're right. I apologize, Clayton." Felicia didn't look at George.

He didn't bother to wait for his father to issue an apology, apparently realizing it would be an exercise in futility. Instead, he took the file from her before turning fully to his father. "What brings you by, Father?"

"I wanted to confirm you'll be at the house for dinner this evening."

Clayton nodded. "Of course. It's been on my calendar for a month. I'll be bringing a guest." He sounded bland, but his watchful gaze seemed to dare George to make an issue out of his statement.

George's gaze contained malicious pleasure when it narrowed on Felicia. "That's fine. I shall warn the housekeeper to set another place...and secure the silver."

Felicia let the comment slide, somehow resisting the urge to retaliate. She prided herself on being mature and responsible, but it was difficult to maintain her dignity in the face of George's unreasoning hatred. It wasn't the first time someone had treated her like she was less than them because of her skin color, but she'd never met anyone so blatant or vitriolic about their prejudices before. To her relief, he departed with only a brief word of parting for Clayton.

Once he had gone, she turned to Clayton. "I assume you were referring to me as your guest?"

"Of course." His smile revealed nothing. "I did say I'm not letting you out of my sight."

She shook her head. "I have no desire to spend an evening in your father's company. I've heard all the insults I can take the past few days. There's no question he doesn't want me there." But that hadn't seemed the case. George had acquiesced without even an argument. His easy acceptance of her at his evening function was disconcerting, considering just how much he hated her.

He put his hand on the small of her back to guide her toward his office. "Relax. There will be others attending, including Mather Sterling. It's about time you put a face with the name, especially since he'll be taking up a corner office by the end of the year."

"If it were just business, I wouldn't hesitate to agree, but I can't do it."

He lifted a brow. "You act like you have a choice in the matter. It's my wish to have you at my side, and my wish is your command."

She had to bite down on her tongue to express her opinion of his attitude. "Yes, sir," she said tightly. "What else is your wish? Should I appear kneeling at your feet?"

"That idea has merit," he said in a smoky tone. "But not for Father's dinner party. A suitable dress will do." Clayton swooped forward, capturing her mouth in a quick kiss that didn't last nearly long enough. As soon as her stiffened muscles relaxed, telling him of her loss of resistance, he withdrew. "In the meantime, I'll settle for coffee and your excellent dictation skills, Ms. Calder."

Before she could retort, Clayton disappeared back into his office, leaving her seething with anger, but having no outlet to express it. She had to settle for tearing the top sheet from her steno pad, shredding it into large pieces, and tossing it at the trashcan before stomping into his office. He could get his own damn coffee.

SHE SHOULD HAVE KNOWN he would think of everything. Felicia grimaced at the box lying on the king-size bed she now shared with Clayton. It represented the end of her only reason for skipping the party. Bearing the name of a famous boutique, it couldn't be anything but a dress for the evening. He had anticipated she either wouldn't have anything suitable, or would try to pretend she didn't, and had countered before she could make that move.

He didn't say a word, nor did he appear to be gloating as he entered the bedroom, holding something at his side. "I took the initiative to order you a gown for this evening, just in case you didn't have anything appropriate."

"So I see." She glared at the offending box, knowing in other circumstances she would have thrilled at wearing something from that designer, especially if it was for a function attended on Clayton's arm. If only things were different...

She cut off the thought with a sigh, knowing she would have to accept things would never be the same again. There could be no naïve delight in the gift, or tonight's outing, because both served another purpose, having little to do with her.

Felicia had spent the afternoon thinking about why Clayton might drag her to a dinner party hosted by his father, concluding he could only be doing it to torture her and annoy George. He could torture her without the fancy accoutrements, but by dressing her up to fit a high-society standard, he was throwing it in George's face that she was trash, strewn in the midst of the beautiful people. For the evening, it was her job to clean up nicely.

"Aren't you going to open it?"

He seemed eager for her reaction, making Felicia's stomach churn with apprehension. What if she had misjudged his intentions? If she opened the box to find a revealing, tasteless dress, it would mean he intended to parade her in front of his friends the way he saw her. What other reason could there be for his anxiousness?

With reluctant fingers, she opened the white bow on the black box, telling herself she wouldn't allow any trace of emotion to cross her face regardless of what she found inside. Despite her determination to remain stoic, she thought she might have smiled briefly upon tracing her fingers over the name embossed on the box with real gold thread.

A gasp of delight escaped her when she lifted out the white dress. It was long, designed to fall to her feet, with a single shoulder strap. Strategically placed sequins gave it a sparkle appropriate for evening wear, but it was a basically a simple design. She knew it would be lovely, giving her an elegant appearance.

Her face fell when she remembered she was to be a tool used to irk George and nothing more. What pleasure she'd felt at seeing the dress faded, leaving a bitter taste in her mouth. She looked up at Clayton. "May I have privacy to prepare, or do you insist on hovering beside me every minute of the day?"

For a second, his expression reflected disappointment. "I'll leave you to it." He set a box on the dresser with a hard thump. "The salesclerk must have included this with the order. I assume it will accent the dress in some manner."

Felicia had the urge to apologize, sensing she might have hurt his feelings. Before she could act on the impulse, he had left the room.

She debated about following him and issuing an apology, but ultimately decided she must have been mistaken. What she had interpreted as disappointment had probably been because she had dashed any hopes he might have had of a pre-party tumble in the massive bed.

A smaller box revealed a pair of silver stilettos that made her gulp at contemplating walking in them. They were higher than any she'd worn before.

Remembering the box he'd dropped on the dresser, she walked over to open it. Her mouth opened in an O of surprise. The salesclerk had excellent taste. He or she had included a pendant on a white-gold chain. A large pearl dominated the pendant, while small diamonds around the diameter emphasized the pearl's luster.

With a shake of her head, she returned the necklace to the dresser, aware that time was ticking away. After a quick shower, she applied makeup, wound her hair into an elegant chignon, and slipped on undergarments. With a shiver of anticipation, she imagined Clayton removing the garter belt and stockings later that night.

The shoes and dress were a perfect fit. To her surprise, the shoes were more comfortable than they'd appeared in the box, though the height was challenging. Upon examining herself in the full-length mirror in his walk-in closet, she decided her original assessment had been correct. The dress was sophisticated, not tawdry, and it made her look suitable for high society.

Felicia returned to the bedroom and removed the necklace from the jeweler's box. Her hands shook so badly that she couldn't fasten the clasp, and she sat on the edge of the bed, breathing deeply. Tonight promised to be an ordeal, but she had to get through it. Nervousness served no productive function. She had to get herself together.

The pep talk did little to ease her nerves, and she still couldn't fasten the necklace. With a long sigh, she got to her feet and left his bedroom, in search of her boss. She found Clayton in the apartment's living room, a crystal glass on the table beside him. He appeared to be in deep thought, and his unguarded expression revealed several emotions she had no time to analyze before he became aware of her presence. His face lost all trace of emotion. "That was fast," he said, getting to his feet.

She shrugged. "I can't get this thing fastened." He walked toward her, and she extended the pendant. Arcs of electricity flared when their hands touched during the transfer, and she had to hold her breath when he stepped behind her to place the necklace.

Once he'd fastened the clasp, he cupped her bared shoulders instead of stepping away. "You look lovely."

"Thank you." She started to step away, but his hands tightened slightly, making her freeze.

"It will drive George crazy," said Clayton, with a hint of amusement. His breath caressed the back of her neck. "Me too." He lowered his hand from her shoulder to cup her breast, thumbing the nipple until it beaded into a hard bud. "As beautiful as you are in this gown, I still can't wait to strip it from you."

Felicia struggled to keep her thoughts focused as he played with her breast. "Clayton..." She moaned when he squeezed the soft globe. "Um, I..." With a cough, she cleared her throat, and her passion-fogged mind. "Do you want to take the time for me to get dressed again later? If not, you'd better stop."

He nibbled on her neck, but his hand fell from her breast. A moment later, he straightened and stepped away. "We should be on our way."

Her lips twitched, but she didn't smile, uncertain how he might take her mirth. With all the misunderstandings between them, he'd probably think she was amused at having some kind of control over him, or at his weakness for her.

A private car took them from his apartment in Midtown East to George's sprawling home in the Upper East Side. The old man wasn't content with an apartment in one of the exclusive buildings overlooking Central Park. Instead, he had purchased the entire building and converted it into a palatial estate suitable for a prince of the past.

As she exited the car in the private parking garage, Felicia admitted the comparison was apt. The Witherspoons had royal lineage that dated back before the Mayflower ever landed. They could trace their patrician roots all the way to the beginning on New England's history and then some. The old bastard still liked to pretend he had the same power over people that his ancestors had wielded. It turned her stomach to know he had that kind of control over her life—or the clout to ruin her life, at least. She had ended up doing almost exactly what George had wanted. His plans hadn't eliminated her from Clayton's life, but they had effectively prevented his son from ever wanting more than sex from the lowly black personal assistant.

Clayton took her arm to lead her into the foyer and through to the salon, where George sat in the center of his court. She rolled her eyes at the way the old man sat in his wheelchair, as though it were a throne. It would be nice to crown him, she thought with a slight giggle. Thankfully, the cacophony of voices in the throng covered the sound before her companion heard.

On his arm, Felicia endured the next hour, meeting countless new people whose names she forgot as soon as they moved to the next group. Her stomach clenched when they finally made it near George, surrounded by several people. She schooled her face into an expressionless mask, though her nerves threatened to make her throw up all over the man's lap.

He greeted Clayton with an incline of his head and didn't spare a glance for her, to her relief. She pasted on a polite smile, the same one she'd used all evening, as Clayton began introducing her to the others surrounding his father. Her attention sharpened when he introduced Lord Mather Sterling. He was a short, stout man, with twinkling eyes full of kindness and a gleaming bald head.

He kissed her hand, to her embarrassment. "Miss Calder, I feel like I already know you." His English accent was familiar, though she hadn't heard it in person before.

She smiled. "I know what you mean, since we've spoken so often."

The next introduction was to Lady Jenna Sterling, a tall, thin woman, probably a decade younger than her husband. Her glossy blonde hair, streaked liberally with gray, was scraped back in a severe bun. She curled her lip and nodded in Felicia's direction.

The last introduction caught her attention—mainly because of the way the woman was staring at Clayton, as though she wanted to devour him. Melinda Sterling was stunning, with a creamy English-rose complexion, pale blue eyes, and silvery blonde hair as thick and glossy as her mother's, but without the strands of gray. Like Felicia, she wore a white dress, but the similarities ended with color. Hers was short and tight, displaying a generous amount of her full bosom and a long expanse of leg. The other woman looked right through her, ignoring the introduction.

Felicia made small talk with Lord Sterling for several minutes, finding he was as warm and pleasant in person as he had always been on the phone and through email. His wife remained at his side without speaking, her gaze wandering around the assemblage, as though looking for something more interesting. Or someone.

With a start, Felicia realized Clayton no longer stood beside her. Melinda was absent too. She cast her gaze around the room, looking for him. From the corner of her eye, she saw Lady Sterling leading Lord Sterling across the room, toward the governor. Her heart hammered in her ears when she found herself alone with George. She steeled herself for a continuation of hostilities.

To her surprise, he waved over a waiter. "Would you like a drink? I imagine you've never tasted Cristal Champagne before."

Her lips tightened at the veiled reference to her supposedly impoverished upbringing, but she didn't retort. In the interest of maintaining peace, she accepted a glass, murmuring her thanks. The beverage was crisp and definitely the finest champagne she'd ever tasted, though she wouldn't admit that to him.

"Tell me, Miss Calder, what do you think of my crystal chandelier? I had it designed specifically to my tastes and imported from Rome."

With a frown, her gaze followed where he pointed. The chandelier was exquisite, and she opened her mouth to tell him so. Instead, her mouth dropped slightly when she saw Clayton on the second-floor balcony, standing close to Melinda. "It's lovely," she said mechanically, unable to tear her gaze from the sight of Melinda curving an arm through Clayton's to bring him nearer.

"Speaking of lovely, they make a lovely couple, don't you think?"

The fine champagne had soured in her mouth, and she set the glass on a passing tray. There was no point in pretending like she didn't know to whom he referred. She shrugged.

"Melinda is a lovely girl, with exquisite breeding. An undeniable asset to Clayton."

Felicia made a noncommittal sound while searching the room for a gracious exit.

"As his wife, she will see to all his needs." The old man laughed, a cold sound that sent shivers down her spine. "A woman like you would no doubt jump at the chance to remain his mistress, but he'll no longer want you after they're married."

Her head spun. "Married?" she whispered.

George nodded, his expression one of smug satisfaction. "It's a key component of the merger. I see Clayton failed to mention that." He laughed.

"Excuse me," she said through clenched teeth, turning from George and rushing blindly through the crowd. Her goal was the exit, but she collided with a solid body before she could reach it. She recognized the body before seeing Clayton's face when she looked up.

"Felicia? Are you okay?"

She pulled away from his solicitous hold. "Fine, but I'd like to leave now."

He frowned. "I saw you alone with my father. I came to rescue you, but I see I didn't make it in time. Did he say something to upset you?"

"Yes." Upset was an understatement. She was wounded to the core, though it was ridiculous to feel that way. Their relationship was little more than anger and sex. He owed her nothing.

Clayton's mouth tightened. "I'll speak to him."

She put a hand on his arm. "No. Just let me leave." *The party, your apartment, and you.*

After a hesitation, he nodded, moving to walk beside her.

"You don't have to leave with me. I'd hate to tear you away from anything."

"It's fine." He put his arm around her waist, looking annoyed when she didn't soften her posture to curve against him. "I've been imagining stripping that dress off you for the past hour."

She made a scoffing sound, but didn't challenge the statement. Instead, she focused on getting through the ride home, maintaining a cool silence. Once they were inside his apartment, she braced herself to withstand his seduction. She might have to sleep with him, but she didn't have to enjoy it. How could she, knowing he was engaged to another woman?

The wedding must have been planned for months, since the merger was almost a year in the making. Before she'd taken George's payoff, Clayton had been interested in her. He would have let their affair proceed to the next level, knowing he was going to marry another woman.

As she marched toward the bedroom, determined to strip off the dress herself, he kept pace. "What the hell is wrong with you?"

"Nothing."

Clayton ran a hand through his hair, mussing it. "Whatever my father said, you shouldn't let it get to you."

She whirled around to face him. "Even if it's the truth?"

He frowned. "I don't know what he said, but I can imagine. If you're embarrassed about your background—"

Rolling her eyes, she turned away, proceeding to the bedroom. "I'm not ashamed of anything I've done, or of my past. My parents were comfortably middle class, not the poverty-stricken trash your father implies." Her shoulders sagged as the surge of anger faded, leaving her on the verge of tears. Not prone to crying, the constantly raw emotions provoking the reaction were distressing.

"If that's not it, then what did he say?"

She looked at him, hoping her expression was impassive. "He told me all about Melinda."

Clayton arched a brow. "What about her?"

"That she's about to be your wife." To her surprise, he laughed. "I'm glad you find it so amusing. You're a hypocrite, Clayton. The entire time I've worked for you, there was never any mention of an engagement, even when we were about to...well, before the situation with George occurred."

With a shake of his head, he approached her, cupping her upper arms. "I'm not marrying her. The wedding is an idea her mother and my father came up with to strengthen the merger. Melinda is perfectly willing, but I'm not."

A flutter of hope flickered through her. "But you've worked so hard to complete the merger. You can't just let it go."

He shrugged. "I would in a second if it meant marrying someone I didn't love. Thankfully, Mather finds the idea amusing, but nothing else. He has said he'd like me for a son-in-law, but would prefer Melinda marry for love, not business."

She sagged forward, into his arms. "I see."

"Do you?" he asked, sounding cryptic. At her frown, he nudged the corner of her mouth with his thumb, encouraging her to smile. "Did my father say anything else to upset you?"

She shook her head, succumbing to him as he led her to the bedroom.

Hours later, she was too tired to move or protest when he lifted her off the bed and carried her through to the bathroom. He took her into the shower, where he washed both of them carefully. Tears burned the back of her eyes at his gentleness, but she blinked them back. It was only her tiredness causing the maudlin reaction. Her emotions were firmly in check, she told herself, and almost believed it.

Chapter Five

THAT NIGHT SEEMED TO have cemented an unspoken truce between them. With surprising ease, they settled into a routine. Clayton was an early riser, and he never failed to have coffee and breakfast waiting for her. They spent their days in the office, their nights in bed, and other times participating in normal activities that couples pursued—socializing with friends, taking weekend trips, shopping, and dining out.

A month passed before she knew it. The realization hit her when she was looking at the appointment calendar for the day. It had been exactly thirty days since Clayton had come to her apartment that first night. With a frown, she counted backward, discovering it had also been at least a week since she'd called Tanja. During that conversation, she had finally confessed to living with Clayton, but hadn't shared the rest of the story with her sister.

Feeling selfish, Felicia reached for the phone on her desk and rang her sister's room. After four rings, the phone clicked and rang once more. A pleasant, restrained voice answered. That it wasn't Tanja caught her off-guard. "Uh, hello. I'm trying to reach Tanja Calder."

"Hold please."

Muzak issued from the phone, and she winced at the volume. Impatiently, Felicia drummed her fingernails on the desk. If she had called while Tanja was in treatment, her voicemail should have answered.

Finally, after what seemed like an interminable wait, the Muzak faded, and a deep male voice answered. "This is Dr. Dareep."

She remembered the clinical director, a short man with coppery skin, and the voice that was so incongruous with his size. "Hello, Dr. Dareep. This is Felicia Calder. I'm trying to get hold of my sister, Tanja."

"She checked out of the clinic about four days ago."

Her stomach clenched. "What?" She must have misheard him.

Dr. Dareep sighed heavily in her ear. "After testing and several treatments, there was no improvement. We determined your sister wasn't a good candidate for the clinical trial, and she chose to leave early."

She shook her head. "No, I don't believe it. She met all the criteria."

"That's true, but she didn't respond to treatment. It was pointless to continue disrupting her life with treatments that weren't going to work."

"I see." Feeling numb, she ended the phone call abruptly, dropping the phone back onto the receiver. Unable to believe what he'd told her, she opened the bottom drawer of her desk to retrieve her cell phone. She must have missed a call from her sister.

The call log showed no calls from Tanja, so she dialed her cell number. Tanja's cheery greeting came on without a ring, indicating the phone was turned off. "Call me as soon as you get this, kiddo."

After hanging up, Felicia sat back, staring hard at her phone as if willing it to ring. Why hadn't Tanja called? Why wasn't she picking up her cell phone? Fear filled her, and she gathered up her things. Something must be wrong. She had to find her sister.

The office phone rang as she was getting up. She snatched it up, rattling off the firm's name. Her heart sank when it wasn't Tanja.

"May I speak with Mr. Witherspoon please?" asked a melodic feminine voice.

Torn between her job and her fear for Tanja, Felicia finally said, "He's unavailable right now." She didn't offer to take a message.

That didn't deter the caller. "Very well. Please tell him the engagement ring he ordered has been resized and is ready for pickup at Tiffany's."

"I'll tell him." On autopilot, she hung up the phone and reached for the message pad. Her hands shook when she wrote down the information, and she practically sprinted from the office. Felicia didn't stop running until she was in the elevator, where she leaned against the wall of the cab and took several deep breaths to keep from crying.

He had lied to her. Clayton had passed off the marriage with Melinda as nothing more than a silly idea of their parents. All along, he'd known he was going to marry her. Her stomach clenched, and she bent forward, ignoring the concerned inquiry of her health from one of her fellow passengers.

At the lobby, she rushed from the elevator and outside the building. It was quick work to hail a taxi, to her relief. She directed the driver to the airport and leaned back against the seat. With unseeing eyes, she stared at the skyline, trying to control her emotions. Where was Tanja? When she found her sister, what was she going to do next? One thing was clear. She could never return to Clayton. It left a bitter taste in her mouth to imagine being anyone's mistress, even the man she loved.

She closed her eyes, unable to hide the truth from herself any longer. At some point, she had fallen hopelessly in love with her boss. It must have been shortly after she went to work for him. Living with him had deepened her emotions, and she had inevitably gotten too involved.

She should have known she couldn't have a physical relationship without an emotional one. Felicia wasn't wired that way. Her previous lovers, all three of them, had been men she cared about deeply. At the time, she'd thought she loved them, but now recognized the emotion had been a pale imitation of how love really felt.

As they neared the exit for the airport, she opened her eyes and forced her thoughts to focus on the task at hand. She had to find Tanja, and Boston seemed like the most logical place to look. Since she lacked a better plan, it would have to do. She couldn't just sit around, helpless and moping, when her sister might be in danger.

CLAYTON SHOOK MATHER'S hand once more as he escorted him from his office. Their respective legal counsel had left several minutes ago, while the men finished talking. The merger was complete. He was in a fantastic mood and ready to celebrate. Planning to have Felicia cancel the afternoon appointments so he could take her to lunch—and then maybe just take her—he froze in mid-step upon realizing she wasn't at her desk.

The logical explanation was a trip to the ladies' room, or she had stepped out to get lunch, but his gut still tightened with dread, remembering the last time he'd found the office empty when he'd been expecting her. Had she gone to her other lover in Boston?

He walked Mather to the elevator, his thoughts on Felicia as he mechanically performed the niceties of parting with him. Clayton returned to his office, his heart racing. There was no proof to suggest she'd gone anywhere. He'd just have to wait a few minutes.

On a hunch, he sat down at her desk and opened the drawer where she kept her purse. A hollow feeling filled his chest when he saw it was gone. Clayton searched on the desk, hoping for a note. His stomach churned when he found a brief message on the notepad: *Melinda's ring is ready at Tiffany's.*

His eyes widened, and he cursed. Having given specific instructions not to leave any messages with his assistant that pertained to the ring, it angered him the jeweler had disregarded his wishes. Now Felicia knew about the engagement ring, which was the last thing he'd wanted.

The phone rang, interrupting his thoughts. He answered it before the first ring had finished. "Felicia?"

"No," said a voice remarkably similar to Felicia's. "I'm trying to reach her though."

"Who is this?" asked Clayton.

"I'm Tanja." At his pause, she added, "Her sister."

He hadn't even known there was a sister. "Of course. She isn't here right now."

"I guessed," she said with a hint of sass. "She's been trying to get hold of me. I had my phone off, 'cause I was with someone." She sounded embarrassed at the admission. "Do you know where she is?"

"No. I haven't seen her since earlier in the morning." Had it really only been a couple of hours ago that she had ushered Mather and his team into the conference room adjacent to his office? She had flashed that lascivious little smile in his direction, the one that always made him want to tear her clothes off and make love to her, regardless of the circumstances. He suspected she knew that and had been torturing him, knowing he couldn't act on the impulse.

Tanja groaned. "Oh, no. I'll bet she's gone to Boston to find me."

"Boston?" He frowned. "Were you in Boston last month?"

"Yeah. That was why she took time off, to get me settled at the clinic. She was supposed to stay with me in Boston, but you needed her." She sounded resentful.

He tugged at his collar, loosening the tie impatiently. "What clinic?"

"You sure don't know much about Felicia, do you, Mr. Witherspoon?" asked the girl sharply. "I'd think somewhere in the past month, you'd have had time to ask a few personal questions between bedroom sessions."

Clayton winced, acknowledging the girl's assessment was accurate. They had talked about many things the past month, but her past hadn't been one of them. He had put an edict on hearing it, and she had obeyed. The truth was he hadn't wanted to know about her sordid history. He couldn't stand to hear the details. In avoiding the subject, he hadn't learned much of anything about her. "I'm sorry," he said, sounding lame even to himself.

"Whatever. Felicia had her heart set on getting me into the clinical trial. She just can't accept there is no cure for my Retinitis Pigmentosa." Her tone softened. "She's overprotective, but I guess she's entitled. Our parents died when I was thirteen, and she was nineteen. She became more like my mother than my sister."

It was odd to hear these details from the sister, instead of his lover. He felt like he was spying on her while she was naked and oblivious to his presence. "That must have been difficult."

"It wasn't easy for either of us. So she's taken it really hard that I couldn't see, and she can't fix it." Tanja sighed. "Honestly, that's why I've put off calling her, because I didn't want her to feel too bad. I messed up though. Now she's probably out looking for me without a clue where I am."

"I'll find her." He sounded more confident than he felt. "I'll start in Boston."

"I'm here in Boston, so you don't need to come all that way."

"I'll be there in a couple of hours." Clayton had to find her. "Where are you?"

"It's a bed and breakfast. The name is Herringbone House. The address—"

Clayton interrupted. "I'm familiar with it."

"Hey, can I ask you something?" She sounded hesitant.

"What?" Please no more guilt trips about how he'd ignored Felicia.

Static buzzed, preventing communication for a moment. When the line cleared, she said, "My phone is dying, but I wanted to know if you're the one who gave Felicia the money for the clinical trial?"

The implication hit Clayton like a fist in the gut. Of course insurance wouldn't cover an experimental treatment. It must have been a costly program, and she would have had myriad expenses related to the treatment. It must have been like a godsend when George made his offer. He groaned.

"Mr. Witherspoon? Was it you? I'm afraid she did something awful to get the money. If she went to a loan shark, she could be in danger."

She had gotten the money from a shark, all right. "She's fine. I gave her the money."

Tanja breathed a sigh of relief into the phone. "That's a relief. I just hope we can find her quickly."

"We will." Clayton shared a goodbye with the girl, but kept hold of the handset. He arranged for his jet with another call, before returning the phone to the cradle. Within the hour, he'd be on his way to Boston. There was only one more stop he had to make first.

Chapter Six

LUCK MUST HAVE FAVORED her, because Felicia had been able to catch a flight to Boston within thirty minutes of her arrival at the airport. The streak of luck held when the plane landed on time, and she had no trouble finding a taxi. She gave the driver the clinic as her destination, having decided to start there. Once settled, she opened her purse and removed the phone to turn it on. Relief swept through her when she saw she'd missed a call from Tanja.

Without bothering to listen to voice mail, she dialed her sister's number. Tanja answered on the first ring. "What are you doing? You scared me half to death."

"Hello, Felicia," said Tanja in a mild tone. "I'm fine, thanks."

She sighed. "Are you okay? The doctor told me you weren't a candidate. We'll find another—"

"No."

"What do you mean 'no'?" She shook her head. "There has to be a program or a cure somewhere."

"No." Tanja sounded resolute. "I'm done living for that. I'm just going to live. If a treatment ever becomes available, I'll take it. In the meantime, why spend half my life chasing after something to fix me?"

"Because you can't see." Frustration made her voice sharper than she'd intended. Softening, she said, "You can't just accept defeat."

"I'm not. I'm being realistic, and I need you to support my choice."

With a groan, she said, "Let's talk about this later. Tell me where you are."

It was Tanja's turn to sound frustrated, apparently. "Not until you agree to stop pursuing treatments for my RP."

She closed her eyes, struggling to comply with her sister's wishes. It was against her nature to just accept her sister's blindness and not try to fix it. Did Tanja have any idea how difficult it would be for her to let go and step back while she walked away from trying to see again?

As perceptive as she was, her sister must know what she was asking would be a challenge. Felicia knew she was an adult, and it was time to let Tanja make her own choices. With a sigh, she said, "Okay. I promise to support your decision."

Tanja sounded happier when she said, "Thank you. I'm at Herringbone House."

She sagged with relief. "Thank goodness you're in the city. Did you get the room with the double beds?" A short silence greeted her. "Tanja?"

"About that... No, I didn't."

Her lucky streak couldn't hold all day. "I hope Mrs. Herringbone has another room free, since that one is taken. You have a room. Do you remember how many suites she has?"

"I think five." Tanja paused again before saying, "Look, sis, I need to tell you something else."

It took every ounce of willpower to stifle her instinctive groan. How could there possibly be anything else to tell her that made her sister sound so apprehensive? "What?" Her voice emerged calm and in control, though she was on edge.

"I don't know if the double room was booked. I chose the Romance Suite."

An inkling of what was to come had Felicia rubbing the bridge of her nose to ward off the forming headache. "Who is he?"

Tanja sounded like an excited teenager, which made her smile. "His name is Brad. We met at the program."

"Is he blind too?"

"He has some vision. The clinical trial was more successful for him, but he won't get any better."

She held her tongue, resisting the urge to point out how difficult a relationship with another visually impaired person could be. Their parents had instilled good values in both of them, and she had done her best to continue raising her sister with those same ideals. It was time to believe she had done a good job and trust Tanja to make the right choices.

"There's something else—"

Felicia cut her off. "Sorry, kiddo, but you'll have to tell me when I arrive. I need to get the driver to change directions. I love you." She hung up and directed the driver to the new destination.

Her eyes burned with moisture when she realized her little sister was truly grown up. It was akin to losing her. Their relationship would never be exactly the same. Tanja would probably come to her for advice from time to time, but she would never really need Felicia to fill the mother role again.

Just don't ask me for relationship advice, kiddo. She exhaled roughly, her mind once more returning to Clayton's betrayal. How melodramatic, she chided herself. It might feel like he'd betrayed her, but he hadn't. There had never been a promise of love or fidelity between them. There was nothing but a huge mess linking them.

The headache had grown in intensity by the time the cab dropped her at Herringbone House. The temptation of pain reliever and a nap beckoned, and she hoped there was a vacancy.

Mrs. Herringbone greeted her with a smile. "Hello again, dear."

She smiled. "Hello. Do you have a room?"

"It's all taken care of." She passed over an old-fashioned key labeled Honeymoon. She recognized it from her previous stay, when Clayton had so highhandedly dragged her back to New York City. With a grimace, she turned toward the stairs. Tanja must have gotten her a room. The only reason she would book the Honeymoon Suite was because there was nothing else. Her little sister had no clue just how much she wanted to avoid ever returning to that room.

Still, there was no choice, short of trolling the city for another room. She didn't want to be far away from Tanja. It was silly to refuse the room just because it would stir memories of Clayton. The key turned smoothly in the lock, and she opened the door. Felicia closed it with her foot, engaging the deadbolt, and dropped her purse on the closest chair. She stretched, rubbing her neck.

"Headache?" asked a familiar voice.

Felicia whipped her head up so quickly it popped. "What are you doing here?" She shook her head. "You know what? I don't care why you're here. I just want you to leave."

Clayton shook his head. "You're not getting rid of me that easily."

She snorted. "Easily? Do you have any idea of the hell you've put me through since you decided I owe you?"

His answer was a surprise. "Yes."

"See, you..." She trailed off when the word penetrated. With narrowed eyes, she asked, "What?"

Clayton stood up from the loveseat and walked toward her. She resisted the urge to back away.

"I had an illuminating conversation with your sister." Clayton hesitated at arm's length away. "It explained a lot, sweetness."

Felicia licked her lips, uncertain how to respond. "Oh."

One side of his mouth quirked. "I'm sorry."

She frowned. "For what?" *For lying about your engagement?* The question remained unuttered.

He ran a hand through his hair. "I made it impossible for you to tell me why you took the money from my father." Clayton shook his head. "It really didn't seem right that you were like that, and I should have listened to my instincts."

Felicia shrugged. "It doesn't matter now."

His eyes widened. "I think it matters a lot. We have to settle some things before we can move forward."

She sat on a chair near the loveseat. "What's the point? This...thing...between us is over. Why rehash all that?"

He flinched. "It isn't over, Felicia."

"I don't care what you do to me, Clayton. It doesn't matter if you give me a bad reference or make sure I never work in this industry again. I will not be your mistress." Her hands trembled, and she squeezed them together. "Regardless of the story you might have heard, I do not have relationships with married men."

"About Marco Trivanni—"

Felicia interrupted him. "I never had a relationship with him. I worked for Marco and his wife. When Marco made his interest known, I resigned. Lana walked in on us when he was trying to undress me without my consent. She offered me a year's salary not to press charges of sexual harassment. I agreed, not wanting to deal with it."

His lips were thin when he asked, "Why did he try to kill himself?"

"I've asked myself that several times." Felicia shook her head. "He came to me, thankfully in public, begging me to be with him. I refused and left him on the subway platform. When I turned on the news later that night, I discovered he'd tried to jump in front of a train, but the conductor stopped in time. He was banged up and admitted to a mental hospital."

She shifted, uncomfortable with the topic and eager to depose it. "Lana called me a few days later to let me know he'd been diagnosed with schizophrenia. His doctor thought he'd been having symptoms for a while. For whatever reason, he fixated on me—not because he really wanted me, but because of his latent mental illness."

Clayton walked from where he'd been standing to her chair. When he knelt down, she tried to resist him taking her hands in his. "I'm sorry you went through that. I understand why you left that job off your résumé." He sighed deeply. "I wish I had been more approachable, that you could have told me the truth—about your sister, Marco Trivanni, everything."

Felicia succeeded in tugging free one hand. "Speaking of truth, why didn't you tell me you were marrying Melinda? I can't believe you lied to me when I asked you."

"I didn't lie to you," he said severely. "At no point will I ever take her as my wife."

That he continued to lie renewed her hurt and anger. Did she even know him at all? His character had seemed better than that. Why continue the charade? "Just admit it. I know about the ring."

"Yes, about that..." Clayton released her hand to fumble in his pocket.

She regarded him quizzically as he removed a small jeweler's box in the familiar robin egg's blue. Surely he didn't plan to show her Melinda's ring? Wasn't he done torturing her? Felicia looked away when he opened the box, but not before catching a glimpse of the sparkling diamond. "I don't want to see that."

"You have to. I need to know if you like it."

Shocked, she turned her head to glare at him. "Who cares if I like your fiancée's ring? Melinda's opinion is the only one that matters."

"Wrong." He picked up her left hand, ignoring her resistance. "The woman meant to wear the ring needs to approve of it."

Felicia froze when he slipped the ring on her finger. "What are you doing?"

"I'm asking you to marry me, in a very awkward way," he said with a sheepish grin.

She shook her head. "Why are you doing this? I don't want her ring." With an angry motion, she tried to tug it off, but his hand settled over hers, preventing her from removing it.

"This ring was never for Melinda, Felicia. I selected it for you last week."

Her eyes widened. "You're joking."

Clayton lifted her left hand, pressing a tender kiss to the palm. "No, I'm not. At some point in the past few months, I've fallen in love with you. The epiphany that I didn't care why you'd done the things you had done, and that I never wanted to let you go, sent me to the jewelry store. I planned to make you my wife, and I wasn't going to take no for an answer." He kissed her hand again. "I'm not going to accept a refusal. You will become my wife."

He had planned to marry her before he knew her reasons for taking the money or the truth about her so-called sordid affair with Marco Trivanni. Clayton had loved her when he had every reason to hate her. Overwhelmed, she said, "Why should I?"

"Because I own you." He put a finger to her lips when she opened her mouth in outrage. "Just as you own me. We belong with each other. We will marry, have many babies, and be the envy of everyone because we are so happy together."

The reality was sinking in. She regarded the diamond, surrounded by small pearls alternating with tiny diamonds, deciding she could accept everything it stood for, and gladly. Happiness made her giddy. "You sure are bossy, Clayton," she teased. With a smile, she added, "I guess I'll have to marry you. You've left me no choice."

"Not in that, sweetness." He leaned forward to kiss her, and she met him halfway. "You may do as you wish in any other matter, so long as you don't leave me."

"Never," she said in a choked voice. Why would she leave the man she loved, who loved her in return? It amazed her that something so beautiful could come from the ugly beginning of their affair. She was going to marry him. It was more than she'd ever dreamed could happen. Her gaze fixed on the ring again, and she sighed with pleasure. "This is so beautiful." Felicia tilted her head. "This ring seems so familiar."

He nodded. "It is from the same designer who made the necklace I gave you the night we went to my father's home."

Felicia's eyes widened. "You picked it out? You said a salesgirl had included it," she said accusingly.

Clayton grimaced. "After your cool reception of the dress I'd chosen, I assumed it would be safer for you not to know I had gotten the necklace."

She blushed. "It never occurred to me that you personally selected the dress. I thought you'd given it to me to wear in order to irritate George that you'd brought someone of my ilk into his social circle." With a smile, she added, "I loved that dress."

He leered. "So did I, especially when it was on the floor."

"You know, the dress made sense, but buying a necklace for me really wasn't the act of an angry boss demanding I repay him with my virtue." She grinned when his cheeks darkened. "Are you embarrassed?"

"No," he said a gruff voice. "I will admit the action wasn't logical, but I saw the necklace and thought of you. I knew it would be luscious with your skin. I wasn't your boss when I bought that. I wasn't even an angry man who'd been cheated. I was a lovesick fool, unable to admit my true feelings, or just why I was so devastated about your actions."

"What are you now?" she asked in a whisper.

"The happiest I've ever been." He took her mouth in a deep kiss. There was a twinkle in his eyes when he lifted his head. "However, I'm also still your boss."

Impulsively, Felicia pushed him backward, sliding off the chair to sit across his thighs. "I think it's my turn to be the boss."

Clayton's wicked grin showed his interest in the idea. "Whatever you say, Felicia."

About Mylia

IF YOU WOULD LIKE TO be the first to hear about new releases, please join my mailing list[1] and receive a free book. I love to hear from readers, so please feel free to email me at authormashton@yahoo.com.

---

1. https://subscribeto.eo.page/myliaashton

Did you love *Desperate Measures*? Then you should read *Cynthia And The Prince* by Mylia Ashton!

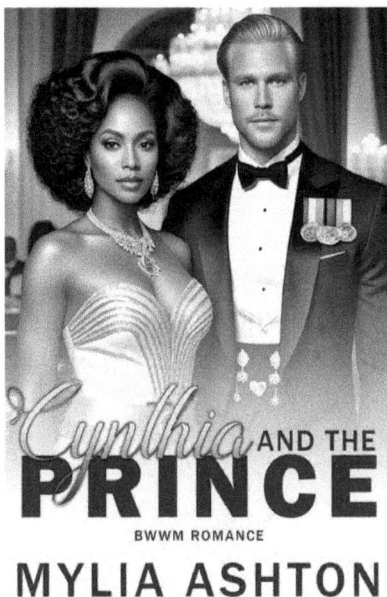

A racecar accident left Prince Logan Arbonnaire of Arganeaux wheelchair-bound. Tough American physical therapist Cynthia Hillsboro tackles the job of getting him walking again despite his bitter resistance to any help. Along the way, they discover a forbidden attraction. Giving in could cost her the career for which she's worked so hard, but how can she turn her back on what she feels for the prince when he so clearly feels the same for her?

Also by Mylia Ashton

9 798224 698035